The Supreme Existence

Previous Books:

Exposed to Winds

Construction Delay Claims

Anecdotes of Would-be Experts

Thoughts in a Maze

Trials and Errors, Laughs & Terrors

Characters

Oddities

Connections

Conclusions Volumes I & II

My Best Dog Days

Investment Fundamentals

Our Support Systems

About My Books

Human Traits & Follies

Honesty's Travesty

Critical Reflections

Us Ordinary Folk

Short Short Stories

Imagined Realities

What if I'm Wrong?

The Supreme Existence

by

Arthur O.R. Thormann

Specfab Industries Ltd.

Edmonton, Alberta

2021

Thormann, Arthur O. R. (Arthur Otto Rudolf), 1934-, author
The Supreme Existence

ISBN 978-1-7770735-1-0

Publisher: Specfab Industries Ltd.
13559 - 123A Avenue
Edmonton, Alberta, Canada
T5L 2Z1
Telephone: 780-454-6396

Publication assistance by

PageMaster.ca

Cover Designs: Front: Image: a Sun emoji
Back: Text by author; image: a snowflake emoji

Questionable Belief:
Why do you believe
In unprovable things
That can only cause grief
As good as it rings?
What if you're wrong?

I dedicate this book to those who believe in The Supreme Existence!

My gratitude also goes to my daughters Nancy & Diana for their valued edits. All mistakes remaining are mine.

Author's Note

I have decided that the book *Conclusions Volume III* must be an abstract of our pure existence, which very much depends on the Supreme Existence, and, therefore, I chose as its main title: *The Supreme Existence*. Since I mentioned The Supreme Existence a number of times in my other books, I decided it would be better to consolidate all commentaries in one book, this one, with additional notes as applicable.

Arthur O.R. Thormann
June 2021

Contents

Introduction

The Supreme Existence consists of inflexible, unsympathetic Universal Laws! Here are some examples:

- Conservation laws;
- Laws of gravitation;
- Laws of chemistry;
- Laws of biology
- Thermodynamics;
- Electromagnetism;
- Photonics;
- Radiation laws; and
- Laws of mechanics.

I have already mentioned Universal Laws in my first published book, titled *Exposed to Winds*:

"I'm where it shines and where it hails,
I am the Law that never fails!
At times, what seems like chaos is
Subject to rules which cannot miss!
Unbending though my rule may be,
You are a short time from it free;
But to save you from eternal loss,
I've built a bridge for you to cross!"

Of course, this bridge is the human mind, which is the only mind fit to deal with Universal Laws; and, discerning what these Laws consist of, and are capable of, human beings can deal with them to their advantage!

Most people refuse, or are incapable, to deal with Universal Laws, and leave such matters to an imaginary God they have created, since this imaginary God is also able to circumvent these Universal Laws to favor His disciples. However, fortunate for humanity, a small number of scientists are willing to tackle these Universal Laws.

Pontius Pilate once asked Jesus: “Quid est veritas?” — “What is Truth?” — after Jesus claimed that he is "witness to the Truth.” Mahatma Gandhi said, “There is no god higher than Truth.” Well, and I tell you that there can be no doubt that the Truth is the fact that the Supreme Existence, namely our Universal Laws, is the Truth that governs us!

God’s Mistakes

The Bible is full of God’s mistakes. A strange story in the Bible goes right back to Genesis (Gen 2:16-17 and 3:1-19). If this story seems fairly straightforward to you, you have missed a number of questionable things; I want to focus on the one thing I consider strangest. The story implies that obeying God's commands is good and disobeying God's commands is evil. I think we can agree on that – and, considering the severity of God's punishment in this story, why not? The strange part of the story is that God seems to have created a catch-22 situation for Adam and Eve: They could not possibly know that disobeying God's command is evil unless they would eat from the tree of the knowledge of good and evil, which was against God's command. In other words, they could only know that disobeying God's command is evil by disobeying God's command! Had Adam and Eve known the difference between good and evil before eating the fruit from this tree, the severe punishment God gave them for disobeying His command would be more understandable. As it is, it is very strange, indeed — a mistake!

With respect to another story, the Flood and Noah's ark (Gen 7:11-12 & 24, Gen 8:3-5 & 13-14), it is hard to determine any exact meaning, either of the length of time the Flood lasted or the number of animals that were taken into the ark. Perhaps it would be best to get an interpreter to let us know if the Flood lasted 40 days, 317 days, or 375 days. A similar confusion exists with respect to the number of pairs of animals that were taken into the ark. However, an even more important question remains unanswered: Was the ark big enough to load Noah and his wife, his sons and their wives, and the various pairs of all species of animals, as well as the food required to feed them for over one year? Noah would have been hard pressed, for example, to get the various species of dinosaurs alone into the ark — another mistake?

Another questionable act involved circumcision. Since God created man in His own image (Genesis 1:27) in other words, uncircumcised, as He must have been, why did He decide subsequently that this was a mistake and required all men to be circumcised? (Genesis 17:10-14)

Also, God inadvertently implanted the belief in witchcraft in the human mind during the days of Moses, when He gave the command, "Thou shalt not suffer a witch to live." (Exodus 22:18)

Prior to the 9th century CE, there was widespread popular belief that witchcraft existed. People saw witches, primarily women, as evil persons, who practiced black magic, but the Catholic Church officially taught that witches did not exist. It was a heresy to say they were real. However, in 1326 CE, the Catholic Church authorized the Inquisition to investigate witchcraft. Then, starting in 1450 CE, Christians engaged in serious witch-hunts, which would last for the following two centuries. To justify the killings, Christianity and its proxy secular institutions deemed witchcraft as being associated to wild Satanic ritual parties in which there was much dancing, orgy sex, and cannibalistic infanticide.

God's Emotions

Can God be predicted? That depends on your idea of God. If your idea of God consists of a Supreme Being in the universe who is governed by and supervises His own laws – the laws that control the universe and everything in it – then, yes, God can be predicted. But if you think of God as some Emotional Being, a Being who can and does disregard or break His own laws, then, no, God will be extremely hard, if at all, to predict.

The idea of an emotional God is not new; it already existed thousands of years ago. Take some references from the Bible:

- "And the *anger* of the Lord was kindled against Moses, and he said, Is not Aaron the Levite thy brother?" (Ex 4:14)
- "And, behold, ye are risen up in your fathers' stead, an increase of sinful men, to augment yet

the *fierce anger* of the Lord toward Israel." (Num 32:14)

- "And ye murmured in your tents, and said, Because the Lord *hated* us, he hath brought us forth out of the land of Egypt, to deliver us into the hand of the Amorites, to *destroy* us." (Deut 1:27)
- "Nevertheless, the Lord thy God would not hearken unto Balaam: but the Lord thy God turned the *curse into a blessing* unto thee, because the Lord thy God loved thee." (Deut 23:5)
- "Then will the Lord be *jealous* for his land, and pity his people." Joel 2:18)
- "And the vine said unto them, Should I leave my wine, which *cheereth* God and man, and go to be promoted over the trees?" Judg 9:13)
- "Then God *sent an evil spirit* between Abimelech and the men of Shechem: and the men of Shechem dealt treacherously with Abimelech:" (Judg 9:23)

As you can see, quite an emotional God is being portrayed for us. If we would change the name of God to a man's or a woman's name, the above descriptions may well fit any one of us. But the point is, when emotions are involved, actions are less predictable.

God's Anti Images

Adolf Hitler, born in Austria to Catholic parents, produced an oil painting in 1913 of Mary and the baby Jesus. Hitler was 24 years old at the time, one year before WWI started. In this painting, he depicted Jesus with blond hair, to portray Him as an Aryan. Hitler's notion was that painters have historically portrayed God as an Aryan, and if Jesus is the son of God, Hitler must unmistakably portray Jesus as an Aryan.

Strange, perhaps even odd, is how churches, especially Christian churches that follow the teachings of the Bible, condone and even promote, all these images. The Bible makes very clear to its devotees that "Thou shalt not make unto thee any graven image, or any likeness of any thing that is in heaven above, or that is in the earth beneath, or that is in the water under the earth: Thou shalt not bow down to them, nor serve them." (Exodus 20:4-5) However, many believers and Christians completely disregard this Second Commandment of God. Christians, especially Catholics, adore images of the Virgin Mary and various Saints, and, sometimes, even request help from these images in their prayers. From a human viewpoint, there appears to be nothing wrong with this, but God may have a different viewpoint, judging by His Second Commandment.

Barbarous People and Gods

The history of fictional gods is wrought with the barbarism of human sacrifices. The Mayas and the Aztecs were particularly prone to human sacrifices to appease their gods. However, human sacrifices are also abundant in the history of other parts in the world, and are even mentioned in the Bible.

Although the Biblical God preferred offerings of sacrificial lambs, He was not averse to offerings of human sacrifices. For example, He asked Abraham to offer his only son Isaac to Him as a sacrifice. Abraham set out to do this, and on the way, Isaac wanted to know where the lamb was to be sacrificed? Instead of answering him, Abraham tied him up and hoisted him onto the alter to be burned. Fortunately for Isaac, an Angel stopped Abraham, and provided him with a ram caught in a bush to be sacrificed.

Such fortune was not the case with Jephthah's daughter. Jephthah led the Israelites in battle against Ammon and, in exchange for defeating the Ammonites, made a vow to God to sacrifice to Him the first person to come to the door to greet him after his victory. When his daughter was the first to come out of the house, he immediately regretted the vow, which would require him to sacrifice his daughter to God; however, Jephthah then carried out his vow.

The most extensive accounts of child sacrifice in the Hebrew Bible refer to those carried out in Gehenna by two kings of Judah, Ahaz and Manasseh of Judah. However, the king of Moab also sacrificed his first-born son (2 Kings 3:26-27).

The Bible mentions quite a number of human sacrifices. In fact, God also sacrifices human beings: For example, Moses said, "This is what the Lord says: 'About midnight I will go throughout Egypt. Every firstborn son in Egypt will die, from the firstborn son of Pharaoh, who sits on the throne, to the firstborn son of the female slave, who is at her hand mill, and all the firstborn of the cattle as well. (Exodus 11:4-5)
Barbarous people and barbarous gods seem to go well together!

God's Sons

God talks about His sons, so, it stands to reason that He also had daughters and a wife or wives — for example, "...the sons of God saw the daughters of men that they were fair; and they took them wives of all which they chose," (Genesis 6:2), and The Acts (14:11) tells us, "The gods are come down to us in the likeness of men."

Furthermore, the sons of God were also fertile: "...when the sons of God came in unto the daughters of men, and they bore children to them, the same became mighty men which were of old, men of renown." (Genesis 6:4)

Too bad the daughters of God were not attracted to the sons of men.

One never knows how much credibility to give to these Bible stories, but the mere thought of gods coming down to Earth via UFOs is certainly exciting, especially when they cohabit with our fair ladies!

Gods as Astronauts

There is some evidence, even in the Bible, that God may have been an Alien Astronaut. The Wikipedia says:

> "Proponents of ancient astronaut theories often maintain that humans are either descendants or creations of beings who landed on Earth thousands of years ago. Mainstream academics, when they comment at all on such proposals, have responded that gaps in contemporary knowledge of the past need not demonstrate that

> such speculative ancient astronaut ideas are a necessary, or even plausible, conclusion to draw."

I have no doubt that God exists, if nowhere else, then in the minds of billions of people. However, the concept of God may have a more plausible basis in reality if aliens were responsible for it. If aliens paid us a visit on Earth and had anything to do with the concept of God and the creation of life, many questionable references in the Bible would start making a lot more sense. For example, we would expect aliens, with the technology to visit Earth, to be definitely superior beings, who may, not surprisingly, also act much like human beings: loving, hating, etc.

The prophet Ezekiel described flying objects (Ezekiel 1:4-27) that could well have been alien spacecraft, according to Josef F. Blumrich, a NASA engineer, in his book *The Spaceships of Ezekiel*. Various civilizations, especially the Chinese, have also recorded descriptions of alien spacecraft. The Dogon people, a Mali tribe in West Africa, claim that they received their astronomical knowledge about the Sirius star system from extraterrestrial visitors to Earth.

Yet, we must ask ourselves, "How likely is it that aliens have, indeed, flown to Earth from outer space, and, if so, from what planetary system?" If we refer to our present technology, we may well doubt the possibility of such a feat; but even if we are sure that visits by aliens were unlikely, we must still examine the evidence of ancient scripts and determine how convincing the explanations are that point to aliens having visited Earth.

I think we can probably rule out space travel to Earth from another star system. However, there is still the possibility of aliens having visited Earth from another of our planets, or from a moon of another of our planets. This poses the question whether or not one of our planets or one of its moons could support life, as we know it. Our astronomers have almost ruled out Mars in this regard, but we must still have a closer look at Jupiter, Saturn, Uranus, Neptune, and their moons. Still, if any of these heavenly bodies has developed an advanced civilization for space travel, we should have at least detected radio signals from them.

The Mystery of God

Many religions portray different concepts of God. You can find the strangest of these concepts in the Old

Testament of the Bible. Here, God is a Superior Being who displays many human traits: He is jealous, angry, partial, loving, impatient, and so on. Therefore, this Superior Being, God, acts differently from what we would expect of a Supreme Existence.

We human beings must learn to differentiate between a Superior Being, a description that fits the Biblical and many religions' God, and the Supreme Existence. The Supreme Existence consists of a set of universal laws, which fairly and impartially govern all matter and life in the universe. These laws do neither consciously and partially cause anyone disadvantages, nor do they consciously and partially give anyone special assistance. Therefore, we should forget about seeking favors of the Supreme Existence; instead, we should endeavor to understand these universal laws and try to live in harmony with them.

If I seem to be criticizing the Bible's God, I am. I believe that God would not want me to act differently. God gave us a brain to use, to criticize illogical situations. How else can we progress and cause improvements? However, you may say, if it is true that God is perfect, He cannot be, or should not be, criticized. That is certainly true, but if historians, such as those who wrote the Bible, portray God as an imperfect being, and if we shy away from criticizing this imperfect being, we, too, become more imperfect.

On the other hand, I would not presume to criticize a perfect being, such as the Supreme Existence.

As long as we are sticking with a Superior Being, we are using our imaginations. However, in the end, we may find that everything in the universe is governed not by a Superior Being but by a set of universal laws – the Supreme Existence, as I like to call It – call It God, if you like, but make sure you leave passion and human shortcomings out of the equation.

Common sense must also tell us that if we are subject to a universal design, governed by immutable laws, we cannot hope to cause alterations to these laws in our favor. W. Somerset Maugham puts it another way in his book *The Explorer* (page 5): "Nature has neither love nor hate…" However, that is exactly what some religions would have us believe, causing us untold confusions, even with respect to our thoughts about the existence of God. Religious leaders have led literally millions, if not billions, of people to believe that God can alter His immutable laws in their favor at a whim. This is nothing more than a hopeful dream.

Let us return to the title of this chapter. If God exists, especially in some human form as the Bible would have us believe, why would He want to remain a mystery, and why would He want us to concoct theories about Him? *That* is the mystery of God!

The Mystery of Life

A set of universal laws, i.e., *The Supreme Existence*, would naturally govern the creation of life, too, which, at present, is another mystery to us. However, I believe that once we solve the mystery of God, we will also solve the mystery of life. Michael Brooks, Ph. D., in his book *13 Things That Don't Make Sense*, delves into the mystery of life, and gives us this comment:

> "Perhaps we are finding life so difficult to make because it isn't as obvious a process as Rasmussen, Venter, and company would like to imagine; perhaps life got established so quickly on Earth not because it is straightforward but because it arrived, ready-formed, from outer space. Though that would make us the descendants of aliens, this is not a particularly contentious idea, scientifically speaking."

The origin of life has to be one of the biggest mysteries still in existence, unless one believes in God's design as held down in the Bible's book of Genesis. For example, to bring man to life, God "breathed into his nostrils the breath of life; and man became a living soul." (Genesis 2:7) However, most scientists and all atheists reject this explanation of the origin of life, without offering us a better one. Scientists can list all the necessary ingredients to support life, but they cannot clarify for us how life got started. The strange thing is this: we can take life away, but we cannot give it, or restore it – simply eating a poisonous mushroom is enough to take a life away.

Perhaps just as certain ingredients, sometimes at a specific temperature, can cause a chemical chain reaction, so could certain other ingredients at some favorable temperature cause the origin of life. In addition, we should consider that finding the answer to the origin of life could simply lie in the ease of removing life. In any case, the trick is to find the right ingredients and the favorable temperature.

Along with the question of the origin of life comes the issue of the multitude and drastic differences of species on Earth, estimated by Professor Richard Dawkins to be approximately ten million. Does Darwin's evolution theory adequately explain this multitude of species? Professor Dawkins does point out, wisely, that the Darwin theory of natural selection has absolutely nothing to do with the origin of life. The origin of life is required for the natural selection and evolution of life forms, but there is where the connection ends. It is inconceivable to me how a crocodile, or a tree for that matter, could develop into a human being. How, then, have these ten million widely different species developed on Earth? Sure, if we already have a humanoid species, we can easily understand further evolution taking place, as explained by Darwin, but this still does not explain how the drastic differences between the various species developed. Not surprising, many people rather believe in the design hypothesis, i.e., God, or some Superior Being, who designed it all. Without an adequate explanation for the origin of life, atheists have a hard time getting rid of the God-design hypothesis.

The Mormon God

The Church of Jesus Christ of Latter-day Saints, the Mormons, have offered us an explanation in their Book of Mormon. The Lord told Nephi:

> "Inasmuch as they [the Lamanites] will not hearken unto thy words they shall be cut off from the presence of the Lord. And behold, they were cut off from his presence. And he had caused the cursing to come upon them, yea, even a sore cursing, because of their iniquity. For behold, they had hardened their hearts against him, that they had become like unto flint; wherefore, as

> they were white, and exceedingly fair and delightsome, that they might not be enticing unto my people the Lord God did cause a skin of blackness to come upon them. And thus saith the Lord God: I will cause that they shall be loathsome unto thy people, save they shall repent of their iniquities. And cursed shall be the seed of him that mixeth with their seed; for they shall be cursed even with the same cursing. And the Lord spake it, and it was done. And because of their cursing which was upon them they did become an idle people, full of mischief and subtlety, and did seek in the wilderness for beasts of prey." (2 Nephi 5:20-24)
>
> And it came to pass that those Lamanites who had united with the Nephites were numbered among the Nephites; and their curse was taken from them, and their skin became white like unto the Nephites; and their young men and their daughters became exceedingly fair, and they were numbered among the Nephites, and were called Nephites." (3 Nephi 2:14-16)

Accordingly, the explanation in the Book of Mormon for the existence of dark-skinned people is that God had caused this condition by a curse for an iniquity, and that God will take the curse away only if the dark-skinned people repent. I will leave it to the reader what connections he or she wishes to make from this explanation.

Nonbelief in God

All these different beliefs make one wonder: How can seven billion people on Planet Earth come up with so many varied and conflicting conclusions about God's existence or nonexistence? How, exactly, do all these believers reach their differing conclusions, and are their conclusions based on facts or fiction? If based on facts, how can they differ so widely?

As already mentioned, the existence of God leads to various conclusions, and there seems to be no factual proof one way or another. Those who believe in the existence of God usually do so unshakably. The same applies to those who do not believe in the existence of God.

On April 22, 2011, I wrote a letter to Richard Dawkins (see below). In fairness, I only got through half of his book *The God Delusion* at the time, but my comments would not have changed after reading the entire book.

Dear Richard Dawkins:

I'm just reading your book *The God Delusion*, and I would like to offer you the

following comments:
There is a set of laws in the Universe, which I shall call *The Supreme Existence* – some people prefer to call it *God*, for short.

If you remove this set of laws, in other words, remove the existence of God, you will also remove gravity and the orbits of the stars and their planets, right down to the orbits of electrons around the protons of their atoms! In other words, you remove the existence of everything, including yourself!

Sorry, Professor Dawkins, but I do not believe you can eliminate the existence of God!

Sincerely,

Arthur O. R. Thormann

Bertrand Russell goes to some length to refute five arguments in favor of the existence of God. These are the arguments he proved false: The First-cause Argument, the Natural-law Argument, the Argument from Design, the Moral Argument for Deity, and the Argument for the Remedying of Injustice. However, he passed over an important argument, to my mind, that is the argument that God exists in the minds of billions of people, right or wrong.

In any case, I believe that one can follow some of the teachings of Christ without having absolute faith in the existence of God, although an argument could be advanced that following the teachings of Christ does not necessarily make one a Christian.

Nevertheless, many so-called Christians, who supposedly also believe in the existence of God, removed themselves far from following the teachings of Christ – especially when it comes to loving their enemies – yet have no problem calling themselves Christians. I am not sure who the truer Christian is: He who tries to follow the teachings of Christ, or he who largely ignores the teachings of Christ, but believes in the existence of God.

I am not saying that we should follow all of the teachings of Christ. Bertrand Russell points out some interesting flaws in Christ's character, teachings, and behavior. One specific example he gives us is Christ's treatment of the fig tree. Christ was hungry, came to a fig tree, found only leaves on it, and said, "Let no fruit grow on you henceforth forever" – despite the fact that fig fruits at that time of year were out of season – and, presently, the fig tree withered away. (Matthew 21:18-19)

Bertrand Russell also criticized Christ for believing in hell, which Russell thought was no longer required of a Christian because of a judgment of the Lords of the Judicial Committee of the British Privy Council on the Appeal of Jenkins v. Cook, from the Arches Court of Canterbury, 16 February 1876.

Bertrand Russell must have been aware of the duality principle that exists throughout the universe (north and south, black and white, positive and negative, and so on). Eliminating one of each pair automatically eliminates the other. Therefore, Bertrand Russell could have argued that by eliminating Satan, we also eliminate God, and by eliminating hell, we eliminate heaven, but he did not use this argument. Instead, he tried to eliminate the existence of God by using other arguments.

In any case, we can advance a strong argument that a belief in God or Satan, or even a belief in Christ being the wisest and best of men, is not required to be a good Christian by following some of Christ's tenets, and the main one of these tenets is "love thy enemy!" From such love, everything else flows.

If you can at least try to love your enemies, that is, attempt to accomplish it, then go ahead and call yourself a Christian; otherwise, forget about it, you have no right to call yourself a Christian!

The Meaning of Life

During the week of November 26, 2017, I asked some of my friends and relatives the question, "What, do you believe, is life's meaning?" The question taken literally could include plant and animal life, in which case the answers might have been "eat to live, and multiply." Note that I did not ask "What, do you believe, is your life's meaning?" About half of my friends and relatives simply ignored the question, perhaps for lack of an answer, perhaps for being too busy to give me an answer. Some said life has no meaning, and most who decided to give me an answer related the question to them and gave me his or her life's personal meaning. Here is one of the answers I received with a religious connotation: "It seems to me that life is a series of lessons, joys, and obstacles, to prepare for the after-life."

Well, there you have it. Religious folks obviously work toward an afterlife. Some folks asked me: "What do you believe life's meaning is?" I gave them an answer similar to what I had written in my poems a few years back:

1971 was an eventful year for me. In business, competition was tough, and we were gearing up for computers to help us reduce our overhead. Personally,

≈

I lost my father. He came through a seemingly successful duodenum operation and later died of heart failure. I had not seen him for twenty-seven years – last, when he was on a short leave from his soldier duties during World War II. I had planned on a trip to Germany for a reunion with him, and I felt bad for having it put off too long. Then, in December, just before Christmas, I was supervising the final connection of a high-voltage installation in a manhole, when undetected ground gas caused an explosion that blinded me for over two weeks. My mind was in turmoil, and my thoughts were challenging life's meaning. Suddenly, on Christmas Day, a seventy-two-line poem came into my mind, and I mean not created line by line, but it just appeared complete. Since I was blinded, I quickly called Renate, my wife, to bring pencil and paper, and I dictated the poem. So often, when we get good ideas and do not write them down immediately, they disappear forever. This is how the poem The Search for Life's Meaning was born. The poem goes through various stages of search for life's meaning and ends: Then, finally, you must give all back, which fell into your hands along the trek: Your possessions, your mind, and even your heart, to give human beings a better start. This action will be your contribution to the cycle of life and its evolution.

The Afterlife

Christians like heaven for their afterlife, and serious sinners are promised to go to hell. When I was a boy, I had an imaginative Sunday school teacher. He described for us children what a wonderful place heaven was like.

Occasionally, the teacher would digress and tell us about the awful place hell. He warned us not to become sinners who would end up there. He said hell was a very hot place and we would surely fry there, and the Devil would come and rub his hands and laugh at us. To stay out of hell, the teacher warned us not to be sinful.

Jewish folk are assured that their souls, that is, the spirits that were with them during their lives on Earth, return to God. This assurance comes from the Bible: "By the sweat of your face you shall eat bread until you return to the ground, for out of it you were taken; you are dust, and to dust you shall return," (Genesis 3:19) "and the spirit returns to God who gave it." (Ecclesiastes 12:7) Well, there you have it. That's where the Jewish people's soul goes after the death of the body, back to God – another imaginative reality.

Hinduists, Jainists, Sikhists, and Buddhists, of course, all want to be reincarnated after death. They want to come back to Earth after they die and give life on Earth another try – either as another human being, or even as some beast or a mosquito. Reincarnation is also called rebirth or transmigration, which is part of the Saṃsāra doctrine of cyclic existence. A belief of rebirth was held by Greek figures like Pythagoras, Socrates, and Plato, and is also a common belief of religions like Spiritism, Theosophy, and Eckankar, as well as many tribal societies around the world. A typical reincarnated figure in our times is the 14th Dalai Lama. Skeptic Carl Sagan asked the Dalai Lama what he would do if a fundamental tenet of his religion (reincarnation) were definitively disproved by science. The Dalai Lama answered, "If science can disprove reincarnation, Tibetan Buddhism would abandon reincarnation..., but it's going to be mighty hard to disprove reincarnation."

Many people, even nonreligious people, believe the soul will continue to live after death of the body. This belief is nothing more than the vanity that makes people want to live forever. These people are so awed by their superior existence that it's hard to believe that their existence will simply cease one day. Thus, they transfer themselves to an imagined reality in order to create the continuance of their Earthly lives.

Here is an afterlife idea I would like to submit to our scientists for assessment: every person has thoughts, and these thoughts might be transmitted into the cosmos by mysterious radio waves, and might eventually be received by another living person – most of us have experienced some form of *déjà vu.* Thus, these thoughts could well become the afterlife of the person who transmitted them. It's a possibility, but it's still in the realm of imagined realities, until its existence can be proven.

Conclusion

There is no doubt in my mind that believers in God like a God who is superior to them, but at the same time almost human. A God who can bend the laws of the Universe to grant them favors. A God who can provide them with a Heaven after death — eternal life, as it were. A God who can smite their enemies!

The fact that all of this might only be wishful thinking does not bother them. They like to play the odds in their favor — just in case there is such a God.

At the same time, they do not mind admitting that our Universal Laws are the Supreme Existence, as long as their God can manipulate and override these Universal Laws! More wishful thinking, of course, but these people don't mind that.

What I Do and Don't Believe

☑ I believe in the Supreme Existence, namely, in our Universal Laws;

☑ I believe in the love Jesus Christ practiced on the cross of Golgotha;

☑ I believe in cause and effect, even though the cause may not be evident;

☑ I do not believe in a whimsical God who grants favors that violate our Universal Laws;

☑ I do not believe in heaven and hell, except the ones existing on Earth;

☑ I believe in the inevitable death of all things and beings, including the entire universe, except our Universal Laws;

☑ I believe in the type of freedom that does no harm to my fellow beings;

☑ I believe democracy could be vastly improved upon, especially the abuse of democracy by a small elite group;

≈

☑ Regarding majority rule: I believe that majorities can be wrong and that minorities are often right;

☑ I believe in each person's right to choose a faith that makes him or her happy;

☑ I believe in the concepts that I'm okay and you're okay;

☑ I believe in criticism, just or unjust;

☑ I believe in music: march music for activities, even for funerals, and tangos for dancing, even at funerals;

☑ I believe most funerals should be happy times, celebrating lives well lived!

The Supreme Existence

≈

About the Author

Both of my parents were Baptists. So, my upbringing included their religion. When I came to Canada in 1951, I was met by relatives who were converted Pentecostalists, except for my grandfather, who remained Lutheran! All my searches for an acceptable religion only convinced me that none of them made any sense as far as their gods were concerned, leaving me with Universal Laws as the Supreme Existence.

www.ingramcontent.com/pod-product-compliance
Lightning Source LLC
Chambersburg PA
CBHW071754020426
42331CB00008B/2311

* 9 7 8 1 7 7 7 0 7 3 5 1 0 *